THE GREAT LITTLE BOOK OF PASTA DISHES

pasta perfect

THE GREAT LITTLE BOOK OF PASTA DISHES

pasta perfect

emma summer

southwater

This edition is published by Southwater

Southwater is an imprint of Anness Publishing Ltd

Hermes House, 88–89 Blackfriars Road, London SE1 8HA
tel. 020 7401 2077; fax 020 7633 9499
www.southwaterbooks.com; info@anness.com

© Anness Publishing Ltd 1996, 2004

UK agent: The Manning Partnership Ltd, 6 The Old Dairy, Melcombe Road, Bath BA2 3LR;
tel. 01225 478444; fax 01225 478440; sales@manning-partnership.co.uk

UK distributor: Grantham Book Services Ltd,
Isaac Newton Way, Alma Park Industrial Estate, Grantham, Lincs NG31 9SD;
tel. 01476 541080; fax 01476 541061; orders@gbs.tbs-ltd.co.uk

North American agent/distributor: National Book Network,
4501 Forbes Boulevard, Suite 200, Lanham, MD 20706;
tel. 301 459 3366; fax 301 429 5746; www.nbnbooks.com

Australian agent/distributor: Pan Macmillan Australia,
Level 18, St Martins Tower, 31 Market St, Sydney, NSW 2000;
tel. 1300 135 113; fax 1300 135 103; customer.service@macmillan.com.au

New Zealand agent/distributor: David Bateman Ltd,
30 Tarndale Grove, Off Bush Road, Albany, Auckland;
tel. (09) 415 7664; fax (09) 415 8892

A CIP catalogue record for this book is available from the British Library.

Publisher Joanna Lorenz
Senior Cookery Editor Linda Fraser
Assistant Editor Emma Brown
Designers Patrick McLeavey & Jo Brewer
Photographers Steve Baxter, Edward Allwright, Amanda Heywood,
David Armstrong, James Duncan & Karl Adamson
Illustrator Anna Koska
Recipes Sarah Gates, Steven Wheeler, Carla Capalbo,
Elizabeth Martin, Catherine Atkinson, Annie Nichols,
Shirley Gill, Maxine Clark & Norma MacMillan

Previously published as *The Little Pasta Cookbook*

1 3 5 7 9 10 8 6 4 2

NOTES

For all recipes, quantities are given in both metric and imperial measures and, where appropriate,
measures are also given in standard cups and spoons. Follow one set, but not a mixture, because they
are not interchangeable.

Standard spoon and cup measures are level.

1 tsp = 5ml, 1 tbsp = 15ml, 1 cup = 250ml/8fl oz

Australian standard tablespoons are 20ml. Australian readers should use 3 tsp in place of 1 tbsp for
measuring small quantities of gelatine, flour, salt, etc.

Medium (US large) eggs are used unless otherwise stated.

Contents

Introduction

Singing the praises of pasta is rather like preaching to the converted; its popularity is phenomenal. Everyone loves pasta, from the toddler tucking into spaghetti hoops to the pensioner seeking a nourishing meal that won't take too long to prepare. Struggling students pig out on pasta; families find it the perfect food for mid-week meals; lovers make a ritual of cooking and eating it together.

Pasta is convenient, easy to cook and very inexpensive. Composed largely of carbohydrate, it provides energy with very little fat. Marathon runners invariably dine on pasta before a big race. Slimmers find it filling, and it can form a very useful part of a calorie controlled diet, so long as any

sauces are sensibly selected. Nor do you have to forego the pleasure of eating pasta if you are unable to tolerate wheat. Pasta made from rice is now available, as are all sorts of pastas made from other grains, including barley, corn and buckwheat.

Dried pasta is an excellent storecupboard ingredient. It has a long shelf life and can swiftly be turned into a meal with a simple sauce based on canned tomatoes or tuna. Fresh pasta is now widely available, and as it freezes well, it is equally convenient.

Pasta comes in an astonishing array of shapes, some of which are described on pages 8 and 9. From tiny stars for adding to soup to large shells for stuffing, there is a pasta shape for every occasion. Serve long thin pasta with a good coating sauce, while twists, quills or shells can take something more chunky. Flat noodles like tagliatelle make the perfect vehicle for a rich creamy sauce.

Some pastas now have subtle flavourings. Spinach and tomato types have been around for some time, but the range has now been extended to include mushroom, asparagus, smoked salmon, chilli, herb and the dramatic black pasta, which owes it colour to squid ink.

It would be easy to overlook oriental pastas. There are so many of these that they could easily fill a book of their own. For a taster, try Chinese egg noodles or cellophane noodles, Japanese udon, or Thai rice flour noodles.

Oriental noodles tend to cook very quickly, so it is vital to follow the instructions on the packet.

Whether you serve pasta with a simple butter or oil dressing, toss it with a sauce, use it in a savoury bake or even a dessert, it is infinitely versatile. This collection of recipes proves the point, ranging as it does from tempting starters like Pasta with Prawns & Feta Cheese to dishes for easy entertaining such as Tagliatelle with Pea Sauce, Asparagus & Broad Beans. Along the way, you'll meet some old favourites, such as Fettuccine all'Alfredo, creamy Spaghetti alla Carbonara and Macaroni Cheese. There are plenty of suggestions for vegetarians, and a tempting selection of simple pasta salads.

7

Familiar Pasta Types

CANNELLONI
These large hollow pipes are usually stuffed, topped with a sauce and grated cheese, then baked. Stuffed par-boiled cannelloni can also be deep fried.

MACARONI (MACCHERONI)
Athough this pasta was originally sold as long narrow tubes, somewhat thicker than spaghetti, the type most popular today is the little curved quick-cooking short-cut or elbow macaroni.

CONCHIGLIE
These shells come in various sizes, the largest being suitable for stuffing. Small ones are good for seafood salads.

FETTUCCINE
Often shaped into nests before packing, these flat ribbon noodles are particularly good with cream sauces.

FUSILLI
These twists or spirals come in various lengths. The short shapes are good with chunky sauces.

LASAGNE
Rectangular sheets of pasta, these are layered with sauces for one of the most popular baked pasta dishes.

CAPPELLINI/CAPPELLI DI ANGELO
Long, very thin pasta that is sometimes dried in coils to keep it from breaking. It takes its name from the Italian word for hair, and the coiled form is also known as angel hair pasta.

MAFALDE
Ruffled edges give these flat noodles an interesting appearance when cooked.

RUOTI
Children often like this wheel-shaped pasta.

8

SPAGHETTI

The name comes from the Italian word for string, a perfect description for the thin pasta strands. Spaghetti comes in a variety of flavours and colours: plain white, pinky-red tomato, green spinach and brown wholemeal. You may also find the white, red and green varieties in mixed packets.

TAGLIATELLE

These flat ribbon noodles made from egg pasta are usually dried in coils to prevent them breaking. A mixture of white and green tagliatelle is sometimes labelled as "paglia e fieno" (straw and hay). Like fettuccine, it's best served with a creamy sauce.

FARFALLE

The word means "butterflies" and the shapes are also referred to as bows, and they come in various sizes.

PENNE

Also known as quills, the term describes hollow pasta, cut on the slant into short lengths. Penne rigate is the ridged form.

TORTELLINI

These small stuffed pasta shapes need little by way of accompaniment, and are best served with either a very simple sauce, or, more usually, just olive oil or a little melted butter. The plainer varieties are sometimes added to soup.

Techniques

HOW MUCH PASTA DO YOU NEED?

Allow 50–75g/2–3oz per person for a starter; 115–175g/4–6oz for a main course which also includes a sauce. If you cook more pasta than you need, rinse the surplus under cold water, drain thoroughly and toss with a little oil. Place in a bowl, cover and leave to cool completely, then chill and use the next day as the basis for a salad, or to add to soup.

COOKING

Bring a large saucepan of salted water to a rapid boil. Add the pasta, stir well, then reduce the heat to keep the water at a rolling boil without allowing it to boil over. Stir the pasta once or twice more during cooking to keep the strands or shapes separate. Dried pasta will require about 8–12 minutes, but fresh pasta cooks far more rapidly and some strands or shapes will be ready as soon as they rise to the surface of the boiling liquid. Filled fresh pasta will take up to 5 minutes to cook.

TESTING

Using a slotted spoon, remove a strand or piece of pasta from the pan. Squeeze it between your fingers. It should break cleanly. The well-known Italian term is *al dente* (to the bite), which means that the pasta should be tender while retaining a degree of texture. As soon as the pasta is ready, drain it thoroughly. If you merely turn off the heat and leave it in the water, it will continue to cook and will rapidly become flabby.

SERVING

Have ready a warmed serving bowl. A large deep bowl is best as it will hold in the heat and give enough room for tossing. Place a knob of butter or a little olive oil in the bowl, add the drained pasta and toss well. If you are adding a creamy sauce omit the butter or oil. If the sauce is chunky, it is a good idea to toss the pasta with a small amount of sauce, then serve it with the remaining sauce piled on top.

TIPS

• Use wholemeal pasta for extra fibre, but cook in plenty of boiling water and check it frequently when cooking as it may absorb more liquid than plain pasta.

• Many cooks swear by adding a dash of oil to the water when cooking pasta. It is not absolutely necessary, but does help to keep the pieces or strands separate and also makes it less likely that the water will boil over.

• Look out for special large pasta pans with integral strainers: the pasta is cooked in an inner, perforated pan which sits inside the main pan. This not only makes draining extremely easy, it also prevents the pasta from sticking to the bottom of the pan during cooking.

• When cooking spaghetti, push the strands gently down into the pan so that they curl into the boiling water as they soften.

• Uncooked fresh pasta freezes well and can be cooked from frozen, although it will take marginally more time. Baked pasta dishes like lasagne also freeze well, but plain cooked pasta is not an ideal candidate, as it can be limp and soggy when thawed.

11

Starters &
Light Lunches

Pasta, Bean & Vegetable Soup

INGREDIENTS

*115g/4oz/¾ cup dried borlotti or black-eyed
beans, soaked overnight in water to cover*
*1.2 litres/2 pints/5 cups unsalted vegetable
or chicken stock*
1 large onion, chopped
1 large garlic clove, finely chopped
2 celery sticks, chopped
½ red pepper, seeded and chopped
400g/14oz can chopped tomatoes
225g/8oz piece of smoked bacon loin
2 courgettes, halved lengthways and sliced
15ml/1 tbsp tomato purée
*75g/3oz/¾ cup tiny dried pasta shapes
for soup*
salt and ground black pepper
shredded fresh basil, to garnish

SERVES 4–6

1 Drain the beans and put them in a large heavy-based saucepan. Add fresh cold water to cover. Bring to the boil, boil hard for 10 minutes, then drain the beans in a colander. Rinse the beans under cold water, return them to the pan and add the stock. Bring to the boil, skimming off any foam that rises to the surface.

2 Add the onion, garlic, celery, red pepper, tomatoes and bacon (in the piece) to the pan.

3 Bring the liquid in the pan back to the boil, lower the heat, cover and simmer for 1½ hours or until the beans are just tender. Lift out the bacon, shred it coarsely with two forks and keep it hot.

4 Add the courgettes and tomato purée to the soup. Season if necessary, though it will probably be unnecessary to add salt. Simmer the soup for 5–8 minutes more, adding the pasta shapes towards the end of cooking so that they cook for no longer than the time suggested on the packet.

5 Stir in the shredded bacon. Serve the soup in heated bowls, with a sprinkling of shredded basil on top of each portion.

Pasta with Prawns & Feta Cheese

INGREDIENTS

*450g / 1lb / 4 cups penne or other dried
pasta shapes*
50g / 2oz / ¼ cup butter
*450g / 1lb medium raw prawns, peeled
and deveined*
6 spring onions
225g / 8oz feta cheese, cubed
small bunch fresh chives, snipped
salt and ground black pepper

SERVES 4

1 Bring a large saucepan of lightly salted water to the boil. Add the pasta and cook for 10–12 minutes or according to the instructions on the packet.

2 Meanwhile melt the butter in a second pan and add the raw prawns. Cook over a moderate heat for a few minutes until they turn pink. Slice the spring onions and stir in. Continue to cook gently for a further minute, stirring occasionally.

3 Add the feta cheese and half of the snipped chives to the prawn mixture. Toss it all lightly together to mix and then season with black pepper. When the pasta is just tender, drain it well, divide it among individual serving dishes and spoon the sauce on top. Serve sprinkled with the remaining chives.

VARIATION

*Other slightly salty cheeses would also be good
– try Caerphilly, Cheshire or Gorgonzola.*

14

Fresh Pea & Ham Soup

INGREDIENTS

115g / 4oz / 1 cup small dried pasta shapes
30ml / 2 tbsp sunflower oil
6 spring onions, chopped
350g / 12oz / 3 cups frozen peas
1.2 litres / 2 pints / 5 cups chicken stock
225g / 8oz raw unsmoked ham or gammon
60ml / 4 tbsp double cream
salt and ground black pepper

SERVES 4

16

1 Bring a large saucepan of lightly salted water to the boil. Add the dried pasta shapes and cook for 10–12 minutes or according to the instructions on the packet, until it is *al dente*. Drain, refresh under cold water to avoid further cooking and drain again. Set the pasta aside until required.

2 Heat the oil in a large heavy-based saucepan. Cook the spring onions for several minutes until soft. Add the frozen peas and the chicken stock and bring to the boil. Lower the heat and simmer for 10 minutes until the mixture becomes very soft.

3 Purée the soup in a blender. Return it to the clean pan. Cut the ham or gammon into short fingers. Add these to the soup and simmer until cooked. Stir in the pasta and heat through gently for 2–3 minutes. Stir in the cream, season to taste, and serve in heated bowls.

Pasta Bows with Smoked Salmon & Dill

INGREDIENTS

450g / 1lb / 4 cups dried pasta bows (farfalle)
50g / 2oz / ¼ cup butter
6 spring onions, sliced
90ml / 6 tbsp dry white wine or vermouth
450ml / ¾ pint / scant 2 cups double cream
freshly grated nutmeg
225g / 8oz smoked salmon
30ml / 2 tbsp chopped fresh dill, plus
a few sprigs to garnish
½ lemon
salt and ground black pepper

SERVES 4

17

1 Bring a large saucepan of lightly salted water to the boil. Add the pasta and cook for 10–12 minutes or according to the instructions on the packet.

2 Heat the butter and fry the spring onions for about 1 minute. Add the wine and boil it away to 30ml/ 2 tbsp. Stir in the cream and add seasoning and nutmeg to taste. Bring to the boil, lower the heat and simmer for 2–3 minutes until slightly thickened.

3 Using a sharp knife, cut the smoked salmon into 2.5cm/1in pieces. Stir the pieces into the sauce along with the chopped dill. Squeeze in a little lemon juice to taste and check the seasoning. Keep the sauce warm until you are ready to serve it.

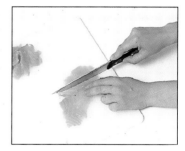

4 When the pasta is just tender, drain it well, toss it with the sauce and divide among heated serving dishes. Serve garnished with dill.

Fettuccine all'Alfredo

INGREDIENTS

450g / 1lb dried fettuccine
25g / 1oz / 2 tbsp butter
210ml / 7fl oz / scant 1 cup double cream
50g / 2oz / ½ cup freshly grated Parmesan
cheese, plus extra to serve
freshly grated nutmeg
salt and ground black pepper
dill sprigs, to garnish

SERVES 4

2 Meanwhile carefully melt the butter in 150ml/5fl oz/⅔ cup of the double cream in a large heavy-based saucepan. Bring the mixture to the boil, then lower the heat and simmer for about 1 minute until slightly thickened.

3 Drain the pasta well, add it to the cream sauce and toss it gently over the heat until all the strands are well coated in the sauce. Add the rest of the cream, with the Parmesan, nutmeg and salt and pepper to taste. Toss again until well coated and heated through. Serve at once, topping each portion with extra grated Parmesan and a sprig of dill.

1 Bring a large saucepan of lightly salted water to the boil. Add the pasta and cook for 10 minutes or for about 2 minutes less than the timing suggested on the packet. The pasta should still be a little firm to the bite (*al dente*) – don't let it overcook.

COOK'S TIP

Fresh fettuccine will cook much more quickly than dried pasta, and is ready as soon as it rises to the surface of the boiling water. When using fresh pasta, cook it at the last minute, after making the cream sauce. Fresh fettuccine is available from most good supermarkets.

18

Spaghetti Olio e Aglio

INGREDIENTS

450g / 1lb dried spaghetti
120ml / 4fl oz / ½ cup olive oil
2 garlic cloves
30ml / 2 tbsp chopped fresh parsley
salt and ground black pepper

SERVES 4

20

1 Bring a large saucepan of lightly salted water to the boil. Add the dried spaghetti and cook for 10–12 minutes, or according to the instructions on the packet, until it is *al dente*.

2 Meanwhile heat the olive oil in a saucepan. Using a sharp knife, peel and chop the garlic on a chopping board. Add it, with a pinch of salt, to the oil. Cook gently, stirring all the time, until the garlic has turned pale gold in colour.

3 As soon as the spaghetti is just tender, drain it well in a sieve and return it to the clean saucepan. Pour over the warm – but not sizzling – garlic and oil and toss gently until all the spaghetti strands are well coated. Add the chopped parsley along with plenty of ground black pepper and salt if required. Finally, thoroughly toss the spaghetti once more before serving.

Pasta Pronto with Parsley Pesto

INGREDIENTS

450g / 1lb / 4 cups dried pasta shapes
75g / 3oz / ¾ cup whole blanched almonds
50g / 2oz / ½ cup flaked almonds
40g / 1½oz / ¾ cup fresh parsley
2 garlic cloves, crushed
45ml / 3 tbsp olive oil
45ml / 3 tbsp lemon juice
5ml / 1 tsp sugar
250ml / 8fl oz / 1 cup boiling water
salt
25g / 1oz / ¼ cup freshly grated Parmesan
cheese, to serve

SERVES 4

1 Bring a large saucepan of lightly salted water to the boil. Add the pasta and cook for about 10–12 minutes or according to the instructions on the packet, until it is *al dente*. Preheat the grill.

2 Keeping them separate, spread out the whole and flaked almonds in a grill pan. Toast them until golden. Set the flaked almonds aside.

3 Chop the parsley finely in a food processor or blender. Add the toasted whole almonds and process to a fine consistency. Add the garlic, olive oil, lemon juice, sugar and boiling water. Process the mixture until well combined.

4 When the pasta is just tender, drain it well and return it to the clean pan. Add half the sauce (the rest of the sauce will keep in a screw-topped jar in the fridge for up to 10 days). Toss gently to coat. Serve at once in heated bowls, topping each portion with a little of the grated Parmesan cheese and a few of the toasted flaked almonds. Extra grated Parmesan cheese can be served separately, if liked.

Vegetarian Dishes

Pasta with Spring Vegetables

INGREDIENTS

115g / 4oz baby leeks, trimmed
225g / 8oz asparagus spears, trimmed
1 small fennel bulb
115g / 4oz broccoli florets, cut into tiny sprigs
115g / 4oz / 1 cup fresh or frozen peas
*350g / 12oz / 3 cups penne or other dried
pasta shapes*
40g / 1½oz / 3 tbsp butter
1 shallot, chopped
45ml / 3 tbsp chopped fresh mixed herbs
300ml / ½ pint / 1¼ cups double cream
salt and ground black pepper
freshly grated Parmesan cheese, to serve

SERVES 4

1 Cut the leeks and asparagus diagonally into 5cm/2in lengths. Trim the fennel bulb and remove any tough outer leaves. Cut the fennel into wedges, leaving the layers attached at the root ends so that the pieces remain intact. Bring two large saucepans of lightly salted water to the boil.

2 Cook all the vegetables separately in one of the pans of water. As soon as each type is tender, transfer it with a slotted spoon to a bowl. Keep all of the vegetables hot. Add the pasta to the second pan of boiling water. Cook for 10–12 minutes or according to the instructions on the packet.

3 Melt the butter in a pan. Add the shallot and cook until softened but not browned. Stir in the herbs and cream. Cook for a few minutes, until slightly thickened.

4 Drain the pasta well, pile it into a heated bowl and add the sauce and cooked vegetables. Season and toss to mix. Serve with the Parmesan.

23

Spinach & Ricotta Conchiglie

INGREDIENTS

350g/12oz large dried conchiglie (shells)
450ml/¾ pint/scant 2 cups passata or
strained puréed canned tomatoes
275g/10oz frozen chopped spinach, thawed
50g/2oz fresh white breadcrumbs
120ml/4fl oz/½ cup milk
60ml/4 tbsp olive oil
225g/8oz/1 cup ricotta cheese
freshly grated nutmeg
1 garlic clove, crushed
2.5ml/½ tsp black olive paste (optional)
25g/1oz/¼ cup freshly grated Parmesan cheese
25g/1oz/⅓ cup pine nuts
salt and ground black pepper

SERVES 4

1 Preheat the oven to 180°C/350°F/Gas 4. Bring a large saucepan of lightly salted water to the boil. Add the pasta and cook for 10–12 minutes or according to the instructions on the packet. Refresh under cold water, drain and set aside.

2 Tip the passata into a nylon sieve set over a bowl. Press it against the sieve to remove excess liquid, then scrape the passata into a separate bowl. Discard the passata liquid, or save it for adding to soups or sauces. Wash the sieve, replace it over the clean bowl and repeat the process with the spinach.

3 Place the bread-crumbs, milk and 45ml/3 tbsp of the olive oil in a food processor or blender. Process to combine, then add the spinach and the ricotta cheese.

Process briefly, then scrape the mixture into a bowl and add the nutmeg and salt and pepper to taste.

4 Add the garlic, remaining olive oil and olive paste (if using) to the pas-sata. Spread the sauce evenly over the bottom of a flameproof dish. Spoon the spinach

mixture into a piping bag fitted with a large plain nozzle and fill the pasta shapes (alternatively, fill with a spoon) and arrange them over the sauce in the dish. Cover the dish with foil and heat through in the oven for 15–20 minutes.

5 Preheat the grill. Remove the foil and scatter the Parmesan cheese and pine nuts over the filled conchiglie. Brown the topping under the grill and serve the dish at once.

Macaroni Cheese

INGREDIENTS

*175g / 6oz / 1½ cups grated Parmesan cheese
or Cheddar, or a combination
40g / 1½oz / ¾ cup fresh white breadcrumbs
450g / 1lb / 4 cups short-cut macaroni or other
dried hollow pasta shapes
flat leaf parsley, to garnish*
BÉCHAMEL SAUCE
*475ml / 16fl oz / 2 cups milk
1 bay leaf
3 mace blades
50g / 2oz / ¼ cup butter
40g / 1½oz / 6 tbsp plain flour*

SERVES 6

26

1 Make the béchamel sauce. In a small saucepan, heat the milk with the bay leaf and mace until just below boiling point. Set aside to infuse for about 30 minutes, then strain.

2 Melt the butter in a saucepan, stir in the flour and cook for 1 minute. Gradually add the flavoured milk, stirring constantly until the sauce boils and thickens. Remove the béchamel sauce from the heat, stir in three quarters of the cheese, then cover closely and set aside until required.

3 Preheat the oven to 200°C/400°F/ Gas 6. Grease a baking dish and sprinkle with half the breadcrumbs. Bring a saucepan of lightly salted water to the boil.

Add the pasta and cook for 7 minutes or according to the instructions on the packet.

4 When the pasta is just tender, drain it well and return it to the clean pan. Reheat the sauce, add it to the pasta and mix together until the pasta is completely coated. Spoon into the prepared dish, sprinkle with the rest of the grated cheese and remaining breadcrumbs and bake for 20 minutes. Garnish with flat leaf parsley and serve.

Pasta Napoletana

INGREDIENTS

450g/1lb mafalde or other dried pasta
basil sprigs, to garnish
freshly grated Parmesan cheese, to serve
NAPOLETANA SAUCE
30ml/2 tbsp olive oil
1 onion, finely chopped
1 carrot, finely diced
1 celery stick, finely diced
900g/2lb ripe red tomatoes or 2 x 400g/
14oz cans chopped tomatoes
1 parsley sprig
pinch of caster sugar
120ml/4fl oz/½ cup dry white wine (optional)
15ml/1 tbsp chopped fresh oregano
salt and ground black pepper

SERVES 4

1 Start by making the sauce. Heat the olive oil in a saucepan and add the onion, carrot and celery. Cook over a gentle heat for 5 minutes until the onion has softened but not coloured.

2 If using fresh tomatoes, chop them roughly with a sharp knife. Add the tomatoes (fresh or canned) to the pan, together with the parsley sprig, caster sugar and wine (if using). Bring to the boil, lower the heat and cook for 45 minutes until very thick, stirring occasionally.

3 Press the sauce through a sieve into a clean pan, or purée it in a food processor or blender and sieve it to remove the seeds. Add seasoning and oregano to taste and reheat the sauce gently.

4 Bring a large saucepan of lightly salted water to the boil. Add the pasta and cook for 10–12 minutes or according to the instructions on the packet. Drain well and toss with the sauce. Serve at once in heated bowls, topping each portion with the grated Parmesan cheese. Garnish with the basil.

Tortellini with Cream, Butter & Cheese

INGREDIENTS

50g / 2oz / ¼ cup butter, plus extra
for greasing
300ml / ½ pint / 1¼ cups double cream
450g / 1lb / 4 cups fresh tortellini
115g / 4oz Parmesan cheese in a piece
freshly grated nutmeg
salt and ground black pepper
fresh oregano, to garnish

SERVES 4–6

1 Grease a flameproof serving dish generously with butter. Bring a large saucepan of lightly salted water to the boil. Melt the butter in a separate pan and stir in the cream. Bring to the boil and cook for 2–3 minutes, stirring until slightly thickened.

2 Cook the tortellini in the boiling water for 3–5 minutes, or according to the instructions on the packet, until it is *al dente*.

3 Grate all of the Parmesan cheese and add three quarters of it to the cream sauce. Stir the sauce frequently with a wooden spoon over a gentle heat, 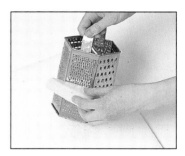 until the cheese has melted. Add the salt, pepper and nutmeg to taste. Preheat the grill to hot.

4 Drain the pasta and spoon it into the dish. Pour the sauce over the top and sprinkle with the rest of the cheese. Grill until golden and garnish with oregano.

Baked Tortellini with Three Cheeses

INGREDIENTS

25g/1oz/2 tbsp butter
450g/1lb/4 cups fresh tortellini
2 eggs
350g/12oz/1½ cups ricotta or curd cheese
25g/1oz/½ cup basil leaves, plus an extra
sprig to garnish
115g/4oz smoked cheese (such as smoked
mozzarella or Cheddar), grated
60ml/4 tbsp freshly grated Parmesan cheese
salt and ground black pepper

SERVES 4–6

1 Preheat the oven to 190°C/375°F/Gas 5. Grease a baking dish with the butter. Bring a large saucepan of lightly salted water to the boil. Add the tortellini and cook for 3–5 minutes or according to the instructions on the packet. Drain well.

2 Beat the eggs with the ricotta or curd cheese in a bowl. Add salt and pepper to taste. Spoon half of the tortellini into the prepared baking dish, then spread half of the the ricotta mixture over the top and cover with half of the basil leaves.

3 Sprinkle with the smoked cheese and the remaining basil leaves. Top with the rest of the tortellini and then spread the remaining ricotta mixture over the top.

4 Sprinkle evenly with the Parmesan cheese. Bake for 35–45 minutes or until golden brown and bubbling. Serve at once, garnished with basil.

Pasta Shells with Tomatoes & Rocket

INGREDIENTS

450g / 1lb / 4 cups pasta shells
45ml / 3 tbsp olive oil
450g / 1lb ripe cherry tomatoes, halved
75g / 3oz / 1½ cups fresh rocket leaves
salt and ground black pepper
freshly shaved Parmesan cheese, to serve

SERVES 4

2 Heat the oil in a large pan, add the cherry tomatoes and cook for about 1 minute. They should only just be heated through and must not disintegrate.

3 When the pasta is just tender, drain it well and add it to the tomatoes with the rocket. Toss gently to mix, taking care that the tomatoes do not break up. Season generously with salt and pepper. Serve immediately with plenty of shaved Parmesan.

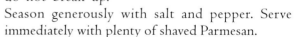

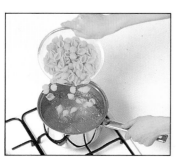

1 Bring a large saucepan of lightly salted water to the boil. Add the pasta and cook for 10–12 minutes or according to the instructions on the packet.

COOK'S TIP

Use a swivel vegetable peeler to shave the Parmesan. If you haven't got a vegetable peeler, you could use a very sharp knife instead to produce fine shavings.

Simple Suppers

Spaghetti alla Carbonara

INGREDIENTS

175g/6oz rindless unsmoked streaky bacon
1 garlic clove, chopped
450g/1lb dried spaghetti
3 eggs, lightly beaten
60ml/4 tbsp freshly grated Parmesan cheese
salt and ground black pepper
small parsley sprigs, to garnish

SERVES 4

3 When the pasta is just tender, drain it quickly and add it to the saucepan containing the diced bacon and garlic. Stir in the lightly beaten eggs, a little salt, plenty of ground black pepper and half the Parmesan cheese. Toss well to mix (the heat from the pasta will cook the eggs to a creamy coating consistency). Serve in heated bowls with the remaining cheese either sprinkled on top or presented separately in a small bowl. Garnish with parsley.

33

1 Using a sharp knife, dice the bacon and place in a saucepan large enough to hold the cooked spaghetti. Heat gently until the bacon fat runs, then add the garlic. Raise the heat to moderate and fry until the bacon is brown. Keep hot until required.

2 Bring a large saucepan of lightly salted water to the boil. Add the pasta and cook for 10–12 minutes or according to the instructions on the packet.

Penne with Aubergines & Mint Pesto

INGREDIENTS

*2 large aubergines, topped, tailed and cut
into short strips
450g/1lb/4 cups penne or other dried
pasta shapes
50g/2oz/½ cup walnut halves, chopped,
plus extra to garnish
MINT PESTO
25g/1oz/½ cup fresh mint
15g/½oz/¼ cup flat leaf parsley
40g/1½oz/scant ½ cup finely grated fresh
Parmesan cheese
2 garlic cloves, roughly chopped
90ml/6 tbsp olive oil
salt and ground black pepper*

SERVES 4

1 Layer the aubergine strips in a colander, strewing each layer with salt. Leave to stand for 30 minutes over a plate to catch any juices. Rinse well in cold water, drain and pat dry on kitchen paper.

2 Make the mint pesto. Combine the mint, parsley, Parmesan and garlic in a food processor or blender. Process the mixture until smooth. With the motor running, add the oil in a steady stream until the mixture forms a thick mayonnaise-style sauce. Add salt and pepper to taste.

3 Bring a large saucepan of lightly salted water to the boil and add the dried pasta, then cook for about 8–10 minutes or according to the instructions on  the packet, until *al dente*. About 3 minutes before the pasta is cooked, add the aubergine to the pan. Stir together to mix well and continue to boil in order to finish cooking the pasta.

4 Once the pasta is cooked, drain it along with the aubergine strips in a sieve or colander, then tip this mixture into a large bowl. Pour in half of the mint pesto and the chopped walnuts. Toss everything together well and serve immediately, topped with the remaining pesto and walnut halves.

COOK'S TIP
Aubergines are available from all good super-markets and greengrocers. They are either oblong or near-round in shape. Prime aubergines have a slight bloom to their shiny tough skin; the meaty flesh is yellow-green.

34

Pasta with Traditional Pesto

INGREDIENTS

1 garlic clove, crushed
25g / 1oz / 1/3 cup pine nuts
115g / 4oz / 1/2 cup curd cheese
25g / 1oz / 1/2 cup parsley sprigs
50g / 2oz / 1 cup fresh basil leaves
30ml / 2 tbsp freshly grated Parmesan cheese
225g / 8oz / 2 cups fusilli (twists) or other
dried pasta shapes
salt and ground black pepper
basil sprigs, to garnish

SERVES 4

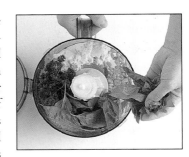

1 First make the pesto. Put the garlic, pine nuts and curd cheese in a food processor or blender. Add half the parsley sprigs and half the basil leaves and process until smooth. Add the grated Parmesan cheese with the remaining parsley sprigs and basil leaves. Process until the herbs are finely chopped. Scrape the pesto into a bowl, add salt and pepper to taste and set aside until required.

2 Bring a large saucepan of lightly salted water to the boil. Add the fusilli or other pasta shapes and cook for 10–12 minutes or according to the instructions on the packet.

3 When the pasta is just tender, drain it very well, return it to the clean pan and add the pesto. Stir the pesto into the pasta taking care to ensure that all the pasta becomes fully coated. Serve in heated bowls, garnished with basil sprigs.

Tagliatelle with Sun-dried Tomatoes

INGREDIENTS

1 garlic clove, crushed
1 celery stick, finely sliced
115g/4oz/1 cup sun-dried tomatoes,
finely chopped
90ml/6 tbsp red wine
8 plum tomatoes, peeled and roughly chopped,
or 400g/14oz can plum tomatoes, chopped
350g/12oz dried tagliatelle
salt and ground black pepper

SERVES 4

1 Mix together the garlic, celery, sun-dried tomatoes and wine in a saucepan. Cook over a gentle heat for 15 minutes, then stir in the chopped plum tomatoes and mix well. Add salt and pepper to taste, and leave the sauce to simmer while you cook the pasta.

2 Bring a large saucepan of lightly salted water to the boil, then add the pasta and cook for about 10–12 minutes or according to the instructions on the packet.

3 When the pasta is just tender, drain it well and return it to the clean pan. Toss the pasta with half the sauce. Serve in heated bowls, topped with the remaining sauce.

37

Baked Vegetable Lasagne

INGREDIENTS

30ml/2 tbsp olive oil
1 onion, very finely chopped
500g/1¼lb tomatoes, chopped
or 2 x 400g/14oz cans chopped tomatoes
75g/3oz/6 tbsp butter
675g/1½lb mushrooms, thinly sliced
2 garlic cloves, crushed
juice of ½ lemon
1 litre/1¾ pints/4 cups béchamel sauce
4-6 tbsp chopped fresh parsley
*175g/6oz/1½ cups freshly grated Parmesan
cheese or Cheddar, or a combination*
12 sheets no pre-cook lasagne
salt and ground black pepper

SERVES 6–8

1 Preheat the oven to 200°C/400°F/Gas 6. Heat the oil in a saucepan. Add the onion and cook for 10 minutes over a gentle heat until softened. Add the chopped tomatoes and cook for 6–8 minutes, stirring frequently. Season with salt and pepper to taste, turn down the heat to the lowest setting and simmer while you cook the mushrooms.

2 Melt half the butter in a frying pan and cook the mushrooms for a few minutes. Add the garlic, lemon juice, and seasoning to taste. Raise the heat and cook until the mushrooms start to brown. Meanwhile, stir the chopped parsley into the béchamel sauce.

3 Assemble the lasagne. Set aside 45ml/3tbsp of the grated cheese for the topping. Spread a fairly thin layer of the béchamel sauce in the bottom of a large shallow baking dish. Cover with a layer of lasagne. Add half of the mushroom mixture, then add a few spoonfuls of béchamel sauce and a sprinkling of cheese. Top with another layer of lasagne, then half of the tomato mixture, then béchamel and cheese as before. Repeat these layers until all the ingredients have been used, finishing with a layer of pasta coated with béchamel. Sprinkle with the reserved grated cheese and dot with the remaining butter. Bake for 30–40 minutes.

Pasta with Bolognese Sauce

INGREDIENTS

65g/2½oz/5 tbsp butter
75g/3oz pancetta or bacon in a piece, diced
1 onion, finely chopped
1 carrot, diced
1 celery stick, finely chopped
225g/8oz lean minced beef
115g/4oz/½ cup chicken livers, trimmed
and roughly chopped
30ml/2 tbsp tomato purée
120ml/4fl oz/½ cup white wine
200ml/7fl oz/scant 1 cup beef stock or water
freshly grated nutmeg
450g/1lb dried tagliatelle or spaghetti
salt and ground black pepper
freshly grated Parmesan cheese, to serve

SERVES 4–6

I Make the Bolognese sauce. Melt 50g/2oz/¼ cup of the butter in a small saucepan. Add the diced bacon and cook for 2–3 minutes until it starts to brown. Add the chopped onion, diced carrot and celery and cook, stirring frequently, until browned.

2 Stir in the beef and brown over a high heat. Stir in the livers and cook for 2–3 minutes, then add the tomato purée, wine and stock or water. Mix well. Season to taste with nutmeg, salt and pepper.

3 Bring the sauce to the boil, lower the heat and simmer for 35 minutes, stirring occasionally.

4 Bring a large pan of lightly salted water to the boil. Add the pasta and cook for 10–12 minutes or according to the instructions on the packet. Drain, return to the pan and toss with the remaining butter. Spoon on to plates and top each portion with some sauce. Serve with Parmesan cheese.

Pasta with Spinach & Anchovy Sauce

INGREDIENTS

900g/2lb fresh spinach or 500g/1¼lb
frozen leaf spinach, thawed
450g/1lb dried cappellini (angel hair pasta)
60ml/4 tbsp olive oil
45ml/3 tbsp pine nuts
2 garlic cloves, crushed
6 drained canned anchovy fillets, chopped
15g/½oz/1 tbsp butter

SERVES 4

1 If using fresh spinach remove any tough stalks, wash the leaves thoroughly and place them in a heavy-based pan with only the water that still clings to the leaves. Cover and cook over a high heat, shaking the pan occasionally, until the spinach is just wilted and is still bright green. Drain. If using frozen spinach, simply drain it thoroughly, pressing out excess moisture. Cut the spinach leaves into strips.

2 Bring a large saucepan of lightly salted water to the boil. Add the pasta and cook for 5–7 minutes or according to the instructions on the packet.

3 Heat the oil in a saucepan and fry the pine nuts until golden. Using a slotted spoon, transfer them to a bowl. Fry the garlic in the oil remaining in the pan until it turns pale golden. Add the drained anchovies and spinach to the pan and continue to cook for 2–3 minutes or until the sauce is heated through. Stir in the pine nuts.

4 When the pasta is just tender, drain it well, pile it into a heated dish and add the butter. Toss to coat. Pour the sauce over the top, fork it through roughly and divide among individual heated serving dishes.

41

Pasta Salads

Tuna Pasta Salad

INGREDIENTS

450g / 1lb ruoti (wheels) or other dried
pasta shapes
60ml / 4 tbsp olive oil
2 x 200g / 7oz cans tuna in oil, drained
and flaked
2 x 400g / 14oz cans cannellini or borlotti
beans, drained
1 small red onion, thinly sliced
2 celery sticks, thinly sliced
juice of 1 lemon
30ml / 2 tbsp chopped fresh parsley
salt and ground black pepper
flat leaf parsley, to garnish

SERVES 6–8

1 Bring a large saucepan of lightly salted water to the boil. Add the pasta and cook for 10–12 minutes or according to the instructions on the packet.

2 When the pasta is just tender, drain it well, rinse it under cold water and drain again. Tip the pasta into a large bowl, add the olive oil and toss to coat. Set aside to cool completely.

3 Add the flaked tuna, beans, onion and celery to the bowl with the cold pasta. Lightly toss together all the ingredients using a wooden spoon, until well mixed.

4 Mix the lemon juice with the parsley. Add to the salad, with salt and pepper to taste, and toss lightly. Cover and leave to stand for at least 1 hour before serving, garnished with the flat leaf parsley.

43

Avocado, Tomato & Mozzarella Pasta Salad

INGREDIENTS

*175g/6oz/1½ cups farfalle (bows) or other
dried pasta shapes
6 ripe red tomatoes
225g/8oz mozzarella cheese
1 large ripe avocado
30ml/2 tbsp pine nuts, toasted
1 basil sprig, to garnish*
DRESSING
*30ml/2 tbsp wine vinegar
5ml/1 tsp balsamic vinegar (optional)
5ml/1 tsp wholegrain mustard
pinch of sugar
90ml/6 tbsp olive oil
30ml/2 tbsp shredded fresh basil
salt and ground black pepper*

SERVES 4

1 Bring a large saucepan of lightly salted water to the boil. Add the pasta and cook for about 10–12 minutes or according to the instructions on the packet. Drain well, rinse under cold water and drain again. Set aside to cool completely.

2 Using a sharp kitchen knife, slice the tomatoes and mozzarella into thin rounds. Cut the avocado in half, then remove the stone and peel off the skin. Slice  the flesh lengthways. Arrange the tomatoes, mozzarella and avocado around the rim of a flat plate, overlapping the slices evenly.

3 Make the dressing. Mix the wine vinegar and the balsamic vinegar, if using, in a bowl with the wholegrain mustard and sugar. Add a little salt and pepper to taste, then gradually whisk in the olive oil using a small whisk or a fork.

4 Add the shredded basil and half the dressing to the pasta. Toss well to coat. Pile the pasta on to the plate in the centre of the avocado, tomato and mozzarella  and drizzle with the remaining dressing. Scatter the pine nuts over the top and garnish with the basil sprig. Serve at once.

44

Tomatoes with Pasta Stuffing

INGREDIENTS

8 large firm tomatoes
115g/4oz/1 cup tiny dried pasta shapes for soup
8 black olives, stoned and finely chopped
45ml/3 tbsp finely chopped mixed fresh herbs
60ml/4 tbsp freshly grated Parmesan cheese
60ml/4 tbsp olive oil
salt and ground black pepper
flat leaf parsley, to garnish

SERVES 4

I Preheat the oven to 190°C/375°F/ Gas 5. Slice the tops neatly off the tomatoes to serve as lids. Trim a thin slice off the bottom of any tomato which will not stand straight. Scoop out the tomato pulp into a sieve, taking care not to break the shells. Stand the shells upside down on kitchen paper to drain, placing the lids next to them.

2 Bring a large saucepan of lightly salted water to the boil. Add the pasta and cook for 2 minutes less than the time suggested on the packet. Drain well and tip into a bowl.

3 Add the olives, mixed herbs and Parmesan cheese to the bowl. Chop the drained tomato pulp and stir into the mixture with the olive oil. Season with plenty of salt and pepper.

4 Using a large spoon, stuff the tomatoes with the filling mixture and replace the lids. Arrange the completed tomatoes in a single layer in a well-oiled baking dish. Bake in the oven for 15–20 minutes. Remove and cool to room temperature before serving with or without the lids, garnished with flat leaf parsley.

Wholewheat Pasta Salad

INGREDIENTS

450g/1lb/4 cups wholewheat fusilli (twists)
or other dried pasta shapes
45ml/3 tbsp olive oil
2 small heads of broccoli, broken into tiny florets
175g/6oz/1½ cups frozen peas
2 carrots, finely chopped
1 red or yellow pepper, seeded and chopped
2 celery sticks, thinly sliced
4 spring onions, finely chopped
1 large tomato, diced
75g/3oz/½ cup stoned black olives
115g/4oz/1 cup diced Cheddar or
mozzarella cheese (optional)
flat leaf parsley, to garnish

DRESSING

45ml/3 tbsp wine or balsamic vinegar,
or a 2:1 mixture
15ml/1 tbsp Dijon mustard
15ml/1 tbsp sesame seeds
10ml/2 tsp chopped mixed fresh herbs,
such as parsley, thyme and basil
60ml/4 tbsp olive oil
salt and ground black pepper

SERVES 8

1 Bring a large saucepan of lightly salted water to the boil. Add the pasta and cook for 10–12 minutes or according to the instructions on the packet.

2 Drain the pasta well, rinse under cold water and drain again. Turn into a large bowl, toss with the olive oil and set aside to cool completely.

3 Boil the broccoli and peas until just tender. Refresh under cold water and drain well. Add to the cold pasta with the carrots, pepper, celery, spring onions, tomato and olives, and mix lightly.

4 Make the dressing by whisking the vinegar, mustard, sesame seeds and herbs in a bowl. Gradually whisk in the olive oil, then add salt and pepper to taste. Add the diced cheese to the salad, if using, then pour over the dressing and toss lightly. Cover and leave to stand for 15 minutes before serving, garnished with flat leaf parsley.

Pasta Salad with Olives

INGREDIENTS

450g / 1lb / 4 cups conchiglie (shells)
60ml / 4 tbsp extra virgin olive oil
10 sun-dried tomatoes, thinly sliced
30ml / 2 tbsp drained capers
115g / 4oz / ⅔ cup black olives, stoned
2 garlic cloves, finely chopped
45ml / 3 tbsp balsamic vinegar
45ml / 3 tbsp chopped fresh parsley
salt and ground black pepper

SERVES 4–6

48

I Bring a large saucepan of lightly salted water to the boil. Add the pasta and cook for 10–12 minutes or according to the instructions on the packet. Drain well, rinse under cold water and drain again. Turn the pasta into a large mixing bowl and add the olive oil. Toss together until the pasta is well coated, then set the pasta aside to cool completely.

2 Place the sun-dried tomatoes in a bowl and pour a little hot water over them. Leave to soak for about 10 minutes, then drain, reserving the soaking liquid. Chop finely and put in a bowl. Add the capers, black olives, garlic and balsamic vinegar.

3 Add the tomato mixture to the pasta, with seasoning to taste. Toss well. Add 30–45ml/2–3 tbsp of the sun-dried tomato soaking water if the salad seems too dry. Toss with the parsley, cover and leave to stand for 15 minutes before serving.

Warm Pasta Salad with Ham, Egg & Asparagus

INGREDIENTS

450g/1lb asparagus spears, trimmed
1 small cooked potato, about 50g/2oz, diced
75ml/5 tbsp olive oil
15ml/1 tbsp lemon juice
10ml/2 tsp Dijon mustard
120ml/4fl oz/½ cup vegetable stock
450g/1lb dried tagliatelle
*225g/8oz sliced cooked ham, 5mm/¼in
thick, cut into fingers*
2 hard-boiled eggs, sliced
salt and ground black pepper
50g/2oz fresh Parmesan cheese, shaved

SERVES 4

1 Cut each asparagus spear in half and place the non-tip halves in a pan of boiling salted water for 12 minutes. Remove with a slotted spoon to a colander, refresh under cold water and drain.

2 Now add the asparagus tips to the pan of boiling water and cook for 6 minutes. Drain and refresh as for the thicker halves.

3 Roughly chop about 150g/5oz of the asparagus thicker halves, place in a food processor or blender and add the potato, oil, lemon juice, mustard and vegetable stock. Process to a smooth dressing. Pour into a jug and add salt and pepper to taste.

4 Bring a large saucepan of lightly salted water to the boil. Add the pasta and cook for 10–12 minutes or according to the instructions on the packet. Drain well,

rinse under cold water and drain again. Turn into a large bowl, add the asparagus dressing and toss to mix. Spoon on to individual plates, topping each portion with ham, hard-boiled eggs and the cooked asparagus tips. Serve with shavings of Parmesan.

Mediterranean Salad with Basil

INGREDIENTS

*225g/8oz/2 cups penne rigate (ridged quills)
or other dried pasta shapes
175g/6oz fine green beans, trimmed
2 large ripe tomatoes, sliced or quartered
50g/2oz/1 cup basil leaves
200g/7oz can tuna in oil, drained and flaked
2 hard-boiled eggs, sliced or quartered
50g/2oz can anchovy fillets, drained
capers and black olives, to serve*

DRESSING
*30ml/2 tbsp white wine vinegar
2 garlic cloves, crushed
2.5ml/½ tsp Dijon mustard
30ml/2 tbsp shredded fresh basil
90ml/6 tbsp extra virgin olive oil
salt and ground black pepper*

SERVES 4

1 Make the dressing. Whisk the vinegar, garlic, mustard and basil in a small bowl. Gradually whisk in the olive oil, then add salt and pepper to taste.

2 Bring a large saucepan of lightly salted water to the boil. Add the pasta and cook for 10–12 minutes or according to the instructions on the packet. Drain well, rinse under cold water and drain again. Turn into a bowl, add 30ml/2 tbsp of the dressing and toss to coat. Set aside to cool completely.

3 Bring a small saucepan of lightly salted water to the boil and add the trimmed green beans. Blanch for 3 minutes so they are crisp to the bite. Remove from the heat and drain, refresh under cold water to prevent further cooking and then drain again.

4 Arrange the tomatoes in the bottom of a shallow salad bowl. Moisten with a little of the remaining dressing and cover with a quarter of the basil leaves. Add the beans, in a neat layer, and moisten them with a little more dressing. Cover with a third of the remaining basil leaves.

5 Spoon the pasta into the bowl, cover with half the remaining basil leaves and arrange the tuna and the hard-boiled eggs on the top. Finally scatter all the anchovies, capers and black olives over the salad. Drizzle the remaining dressing over the top and garnish with the remaining basil leaves. Serve.

Easy Entertaining

Fettuccine with Saffron Mussels

INGREDIENTS

*1.75kg/4-4½lb fresh mussels, scrubbed
and bearded
2 shallots, chopped
150ml/¼ pint/⅔ cup dry white wine
generous pinch of saffron strands
350g/12oz dried fettuccine
25g/1oz/2 tbsp butter
2 garlic cloves, crushed
250ml/8fl oz/1 cup double cream
1 egg yolk
salt and ground black pepper
30ml/2 tbsp chopped fresh parsley, to garnish*

SERVES 4

1 Place the mussels in a large saucepan. Add the shallots and wine. Cover tightly and cook over a high heat for 5–8 minutes, shaking the pan frequently, until the mussels have opened. Using a slotted spoon, remove the mussels from the pan. Discard any mussels that have not opened during the cooking process. Set aside a few of the mussels in their shells for garnishing; shell the rest and keep them hot until required.

2 Bring the cooking liquid remaining in the saucepan to the boil. Cook until it has reduced by half, then strain it into a jug, stir in the saffron strands and set aside.

3 Bring a large saucepan of lightly salted water to the boil. Add the pasta and cook for 10–12 minutes or according to the instructions on the packet.

4 Meanwhile melt the butter in a frying pan. Cook the garlic over a low heat for 1 minute, then pour in the saffron-flavoured mussel liquid and the cream. Heat gently until the sauce starts to thicken, then remove the pan from the heat and stir in the egg yolk and shelled mussels. Season to taste.

5 When tender, drain and season the pasta, then divide among serving plates. Spoon over the sauce and garnish with parsley and the reserved mussels.

Cannelloni al Forno

INGREDIENTS

15g / ½oz / 1 tbsp butter
450g / 1lb boned and skinned chicken
breasts, cooked
225g / 8oz mushrooms, trimmed and halved
2 garlic cloves, crushed
30ml / 2 tbsp chopped fresh parsley
15ml / 1 tbsp chopped fresh tarragon
1 egg, beaten
lemon juice (see method)
12–18 dried cannelloni tubes
600ml / 1 pint / 2½ cups Napoletana sauce
50g / 2oz / ½ cup freshly grated Parmesan cheese
salt and ground black pepper
flat leaf parsley sprigs, to garnish

SERVES 4–6

1 Preheat the oven to 200°C/400°F/Gas 6. Using the butter, generously grease a baking dish or shallow casserole large enough to hold all the cannelloni in a single layer. Chop the chicken roughly, then place it in a food processor fitted with a metal blade and chop it very finely. Scrape into a mixing bowl and set aside until required.

2 Add the mushrooms, garlic, parsley and tarragon to the food processor and process finely. Add to the chicken, then stir in the egg. Season with salt and pepper and add a dash or two of lemon juice.

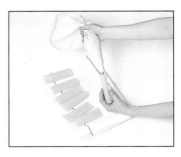

3 Cook the cannelloni in boiling water if necessary (check the instructions on the packet) and drain well. Spoon the chicken mixture into a piping bag fitted with a large plain nozzle and fill the cannelloni tubes. Alternatively, fill the tubes with a spoon.

4 Put the tubes in the dish or casserole. Spoon over the sauce and sprinkle with the cheese. Bake for 30 minutes, until golden. Garnish with parsley.

COOK'S TIP

Mushrooms are sold either as buttons, cups or flats according to age. Use mushrooms on the day of purchase as they don't store well and go limp and lose their flavour quickly.

Tagliatelle with Gorgonzola Sauce

INGREDIENTS

450g/1lb dried tagliatelle
5ml/1 tsp cornflour
30ml/2 tbsp dry vermouth
25g/1oz/2 tbsp butter, plus extra for
tossing the pasta
225g/8oz Gorgonzola cheese
150ml/5fl oz/⅔ cup double or whipping cream
15ml/1 tbsp chopped fresh sage
salt and ground black pepper

SERVES 4

1 Bring a large saucepan of lightly salted water to the boil. Add the pasta and cook for 10–12 minutes or according to the instructions on the packet.

2 Mix the cornflour with the vermouth in a cup. Melt the butter in a heavy-based saucepan. Crumble in 175g/6oz of the Gorgonzola and stir over a very gentle heat until the cheese melts. Pour in the cream, then whisk in the cornflour mixture. Stir in the sage, with salt and pepper to taste. Cook, whisking constantly, until the sauce thickens, then remove the pan from the heat.

3 When the pasta is tender, drain it, pile it into a large heated dish and toss in a knob of butter.

4 If it is necessary, reheat and whisk the sauce. Serve the pasta in heated bowls, topping each portion with sauce and the remaining cheese, crumbled on top.

Spaghetti with Seafood Sauce

INGREDIENTS

45ml/3 tbsp olive oil
1 onion, chopped
1 garlic clove, crushed
225g/8oz dried spaghetti
600ml/1 pint/2½ cups passata or strained,
puréed canned tomatoes
15ml/1 tbsp tomato purée
5ml/1 tsp dried oregano
1 bay leaf
5ml/1 tsp sugar
115g/4oz cooked prawns, peeled and deveined
175g/6oz/1½ cups cooked clam or cockle meat
(rinsed and drained if canned or bottled)
15ml/1 tbsp lemon juice
45ml/3 tbsp chopped fresh parsley
25g/1oz/2 tbsp butter
salt and ground black pepper
4 whole cooked prawns, to garnish (optional)

SERVES 4

1 Heat the oil in a saucepan. Add the onion and garlic. Cook over a moderate heat for 6–7 minutes, until the onion has softened.

2 Meanwhile bring a large saucepan of lightly salted water to the boil. Add the dried spaghetti and cook for 10–12 minutes, or according to the instructions on the packet, until it is *al dente*.

3 Stir the passata or strained tomatoes into the onion. Add the tomato purée, oregano, bay leaf and sugar. Bring to the boil, then lower the heat and simmer for 2–3 minutes. Stir in the shellfish, lemon juice and two thirds of the parsley. Cover and cook for 6–7 minutes. Season to taste.

4 When the spaghetti is just tender, drain it well and return it to the clean pan. Add the butter and toss until completely coated. Divide the spaghetti among four heated bowls and top with the seafood sauce. Garnish with the remaining parsley and the whole prawns, if using.

Prawns with Pasta & Pesto in Packets

INGREDIENTS

750g / 1½lb whole medium raw prawns
450g / 1lb tagliatelle or similar pasta
150ml / 5fl oz / ⅔ cup fresh pesto sauce or
ready-made equivalent
20ml / 4 tsp olive oil
1 garlic clove, crushed
100ml / 4fl oz / ½ cup dry white wine
salt and ground black pepper

SERVES 4

58

1 Preheat the oven to 200°C/400°F/Gas 6. Twist the heads off the prawns and discard.

2 Cook the pasta in plenty of boiling salted water for 2 minutes, then drain. Mix with half the pesto.

3 Cut four 30cm/12in squares of greaseproof paper and put 5ml/1 tsp olive oil in the centre of each. Pile equal amounts of the pasta mixture in the middle of each square.

4 Top each square with prawns and spoon the remaining pesto, mixed with the garlic, over the top. Season with pepper and sprinkle the wine among them.

5 Brush the edges of the paper lightly with water and bring them loosely up around the filling, twisting them tightly to enclose the filling.

6 Place the parcels on a baking sheet and bake for 10–15 minutes. Serve them immediately, allowing each person to open his or her own pasta packet.

COOK'S TIP
Try using other fresh fish and seafood instead of prawns, if you prefer.

Linguine with Prosciutto & Parmesan

INGREDIENTS

115g/4oz prosciutto
450g/1lb dried linguine
75g/3oz/6 tbsp butter
50g/2oz/½ cup freshly grated Parmesan cheese
salt and ground black pepper
a few fresh sage leaves, to garnish

SERVES 4

I Using a sharp knife, cut the prosciutto into strips the same width as the linguine. Bring a large saucepan of lightly salted water to the boil. Add the linguine and cook for 10–12 minutes, or according to the instructions on the packet, until it is *al dente*.

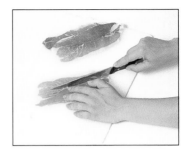

2 Meanwhile melt the butter gently in a second small saucepan. Stir in all the prosciutto strips and heat them through gently, taking care not to fry them.

3 When the linguine is ready, drain it well then divide it among four individual heated serving plates. Sprinkle the Parmesan cheese over the top, then pour over the buttery prosciutto strips and season with plenty of black pepper. (Since the cheese is salty, salt need not be added.) Serve at once, garnished with the sage leaves. You may also like to serve this dish with some additional grated Parmesan cheese in a separate, small serving bowl.

Spaghetti with Black Olive & Mushroom Sauce

INGREDIENTS

15ml / 1 tbsp olive oil
1 garlic clove, chopped
225g / 8oz mushrooms, chopped
150g / 5oz / ⅔ cups stoned black olives
30ml / 2 tbsp chopped fresh parsley
1 red chilli, seeded and chopped
450g / 1lb dried spaghetti
225g / 8oz cherry tomatoes
slivers of Parmesan cheese, to garnish

SERVES 4

1 Heat the oil in a large saucepan and cook the garlic over a gentle heat for 1 minute. Add the mushrooms, raise the heat a little and cover. Cook for 5 minutes.

2 Tip the mushroom mixture into a food processor or blender. Add the olives, parsley and chilli. Process until smooth, then scrape into a bowl and set aside. Bring a large saucepan of lightly salted water to the boil. Add the spaghetti and cook for 10–12 minutes, or according to the instructions on the packet, until it is *al dente*.

3 Meanwhile heat an ungreased frying pan, add the cherry tomatoes and shake the pan over a moderate heat for 2–3 minutes until the skins start to split.

4 Drain the pasta, return it to the clean pan and add the olive mixture. Toss to coat. Serve the pasta topped with the tomatoes and garnished with the Parmesan.

61

Tagliatelle with Pea Sauce, Asparagus & Broad Beans

INGREDIENTS

15ml / 1 tbsp olive oil
1 garlic clove, crushed
6 spring onions, thinly sliced
225g / 8oz / 2 cups frozen peas, thawed
350g / 12oz young asparagus spears
30ml / 2 tbsp chopped fresh sage, plus extra
leaves to garnish
finely grated rind of 2 lemons
450ml / ¾ pint / scant 2 cups vegetable stock
225g / 8oz frozen broad beans, thawed
450g / 1lb dried tagliatelle
60ml / 4 tbsp natural yogurt
salt and ground black pepper

SERVES 4

I Heat the oil in a large pan. Add the garlic and spring onions and cook gently for about 2–3 minutes. Stir in the peas and one third of the asparagus, with all the chopped sage, lemon rind and stock or water. Simmer for 10 minutes, until the asparagus is tender. Purée in a food processor or blender until smooth, then return the sauce to the clean pan.

2 Pinch the broad beans between your fingers to pop off the skins, revealing the tender green beans. Discard the skins. Bring a small pan of water to the boil. Cut the remaining asparagus into 5cm/2in lengths, add it to the boiling water and cook until just tender. Drain well.

3 Bring a large pan of lightly salted water to the boil. Add the pasta and cook for 10–12 minutes or according to the instructions on the packet.

4 Add the cooked asparagus and the beans to the pea sauce. Stir in the yogurt and reheat gently – do not allow the sauce to boil. Season with salt and pepper.

5 When the pasta is just tender, drain it well and divide it among heated serving plates. Spoon the pea sauce over the pasta, garnish with some fresh sage, and serve at once.

Index